ALWAYS DANGER

CRAB ORCHARD SERIES IN POETRY

OPEN COMPETITION AWARD

ALWAYS DANGER

DAVID HERNANDEZ

Crab Orchard Review

&

Southern Illinois University Press

CARBONDALE

09   08   07   06   4   3   2   1

The Crab Orchard Series in Poetry is a joint publishing venture
of Southern Illinois University Press and *Crab Orchard Review.*
This series has been made possible by the generous support of the
Office of the President of Southern Illinois University and the
Office of the Vice Chancellor for Academic Affairs and Provost at
Southern Illinois University Carbondale.

Crab Orchard Series in Poetry Editor: Jon Tribble
Open Competition Award Judge for 2005: Leslie Adrienne Miller

Library of Congress Cataloging-in-Publication Data
Hernandez, David, 1971–
   Always danger / David Hernandez.
      p. cm. — (Crab Orchard series in poetry)
I. Title. II. Series: Crab Orchard award series in poetry.
PS3608.E766A49 2006
813'.6—dc22
ISBN 0-8093-2691-4
ISBN 978-0-8093-2691-4   2005027337

Printed on recycled paper. ♻

The paper used in this publication meets the minimum
requirements of American National Standard for Information
Sciences—Permanence of Paper for Printed Library Materials,
ANSI Z39.48-1992. ⊚

FOR LISA

CONTENTS

ACKNOWLEDGMENTS

Thanks to the editors of the following publications, in which poems in this collection first appeared:

Agni—"Damage"
Alaska Quarterly Review—"Driving Toward the Sun"
Bloomsbury Review—"Night"
Crab Orchard Review—"Always Danger"
Epoch—"Episode"
5 AM—"Disappearer" and "Self-Portrait with Back Turned"
Green Mountains Review—"The Circus Octopus"
Iowa Review—"The Goldfish"
Luna—"The Grandfather" and "Humiliating the Tyrants"
MiPO—"So the Pilot Says Over the Intercom"
Mississippi Review—"The Taxicab Incident"
Missouri Review—"Bully," "Donut Shop," "Leaving the Nurse," and "The Soldier Inside the Horse"
North American Review—"Man on an Island"
Pearl—"Another Dimension," "Dumbest," and "The Gondolier"
Pleiades—"Bullet"
Ploughshares—"Chess Match Ends in Fight"
Poet Lore—"The Dinner Party"
Poetry International—"According to One Statistic" and "How to Commit Adultery"
Pool—"Razors"
Prairie Schooner—"A Brief History of Antidepressants"
Quarterly West—"The Sad Punk" and "A Story to Tell"
Shade—"The Eyes"
Slipstream—"Ghost Brother"
Slope—"Customer Lounge" and "Subzero"
The Southern Review—"Appointment"
Sycamore Review—"Alzheimer's" and "Balcony Talk with Cigars"

TriQuarterly—"Portrait of My Father Slapping His Ear" and
  "What a Little Charisma Can Do"
West Branch—"Fontanelle"

"How to Commit Adultery" was also reprinted in
Homewrecker: An Adultery Anthology, edited by Daphne
Gottlieb (Soft Skull Press, 2005).

"The Whirling Funnel" was printed as a limited edition broad-
side by Fameorshame Press (2005).

ONE

There's a one-armed man on a hill
eating a candy bar and we wonder

which war, what factory machine.
Looks like his shoulder's gone too.

Looks like the sky is a blue curtain
closing in on him. There's a cloud

gliding into his rib. There's his hand
rising to his mouth, teeth grinding

chocolate, the gift of sugar his lone
hand keeps delivering to his mouth.

Whatever happened, he's moved on,
wakes, showers and buttons his shirt

by himself, his hand a swan pecking
down his chest. Wakes from a dream

where his missing arm flies into
his sleeve to pay his body a visit.

Wakes and buttons down and buys
a candy bar at the store. Damage

makes a notch on us all, with some
another notch. With some it steadies

the chisel and brings the hammer
down quick, brings a lesson on loss.

Blades take fingers. A tractor makes
a girl say goodbye to her footprints.

As for the one-armed man on the hill,
looks like the candy bar's gone.

He looks like a sculpture, standing
up there with a hand on his waist:

a general waiting for the enemy,
hiding his saber behind his back.

THE SOLDIER INSIDE THE HORSE

for Anthony

A horse disemboweled on a battlefield
for the soldier to crawl inside.

A battlefield once green, once shagged
with bluegrass, now gouged and smoldering.

The soldier once a boy and now
a man inside a horse hollowed out.

The horse then the soldier's costume,
the mouth an opening for his rifle

and not a mouth chewing the bluegrass.
Once the eye sockets cradled eyes

and now peepholes for the soldier
to survey the battlefield, smoldering

and gouged. Once green, once a boy
with strawberry jelly on his lips.

Once a ghost for Halloween with eyeholes
scissored into a bedsheet. An enemy

crosses the battlefield so gunfire
from the mouth of the horse,

so death. The man inside a soldier,
the soldier once a boy who wanted

a pony. The horse once a horse,
galloping where the world was green.

I know a girl thirteen and lean
as a sunflower stalk, all blunt

angles and bones, a girl who
never removes her necklace,

a black string of shark teeth.
To school and home, to shower

and sleep—always the comfort
of those incisors resting against

collarbone. Between classes
she slips her narrow body

through crammed hallways,
around jutting backpacks, elbows.

Home, whatever's spooned
onto her plate she nibbles with

her small teeth, her larger pair
dangling above the untouched

potatoes. Only one finger's
needed to empty her stomach,

one to flush before she showers,
water lacquering her skin, water

climbing down the twelve rungs
of ribcage. Off to sleep, barely

a mound under the covers,
barely the rise and fall of breathing

as her necklace etches her flesh,
checkmarks over her heart.

CUSTOMER LOUNGE

The old woman hauled her bones
here, where they hoist our cars,

where they tinker with their guts.
She can't sit still. Up, toward

the sun-washed window, back
to her orange chair, up again.

The air-conditioner rattles,
ball of phlegm in its throat.

Everything falls apart, needs repair.
She knits and the pink spreads

across her lap. Sweater or shawl,
time will unravel it, a moth will build

a hole there. You can even hear
her breathing coming undone,

its rusted bolts squeaking free.
Static on the intercom, then a name.

The old woman gets up, pays,
and hobbles out into the afternoon

where a mechanic curses,
fixing what cannot be fixed.

ALZHEIMER'S

In the photograph she's knitting
and the crow is perched on her lap.

Two decades away from her brain's
unraveling and the bird has the yarn

in its beak, its wings two waterfalls
except water isn't falling but something

darker. Think nightfalls, shadowfalls.
Around her finger a yellow ring

of thread as she purls and knits
herself a sweater, her brain's erasing

two decades away. I'm just a boy.
I believe the crow will unknit

the morning's work, will tug the yarn
dangling wormlike in its beak.

Now, two decades later, the photo's
in my hands. Now she wants to see

her parents and says with frequency
I want to see my parents now

although decades ago the earth
crumbled her parents in its hands.

Sometimes she shoos away her illness
and stitches with language a name

or a place we recognize. Sometimes,
before her mind's tugged and comes

undone, she says *Santiago* and sees
blue sky, the blue mountains

of the Andes eclipsing the stars.
Sees wind, troubling the bluegrass.

To run away from home with hands
empty and hop a train ticketless

but meet a stranger kind enough
to hide a boy for miles under the tent

his poncho makes as they sway
up the coast of Chile to wherever

it was the tracks were laid and spiked
into the earth. To feed his hands

to a mine shaft and cut through
its darkness with a light blazing

from his hardhat and clock out
wearing grime's shadow on his face.

Hands scraped raw as he toppled
down the Andes alone at twilight

with anguished knees and believed
the lowering night was the lid

to his coffin. How one hand shook
Kennedy's in an elevator and how

in those brief seconds as the lit floors
chimed backwards his greatness

was tangible. How this same hand
curled around a closed umbrella

as he swung it down and down again
in a gesture known as violence

against his daughter bleating on her bed.
To have lived during ninety-one

percent of last century's progress
and horrors and to breathe now

in this one in a hospital room
with his wife sedated on another bed

with an IV plugged into her wrist
and in a gesture recognized as kindness

smoothes over her silver tresses
using a hand veined with blue rivers.

THE TAXICAB INCIDENT

A boy runs into a busy street,
a boy who happens to be my father.
Yes he's careless and yes here comes
the taxicab. This happened
in Bogotá, Colombia. And this:

a boy falls, a boy who happens
to be my father, fallen before
the taxicab. You know what
happens next: my existence
spoils the drama. How the taxicab

glides over my father and skims
his shoulder blades. He stands
unscathed and brushes the dust off
his clothes and continues to breathe.
Fallen differently, I'm not here.

Fallen the way he did, I am.
When the boy who happens to be
my father runs into a busy street,
I'm in the backseat of that taxicab
with my brother and sister.

The three of us, we're outlined.
Our skin is translucent as cellophane.
When we begin to scream
nothing but nothing leaps
from the zeros of our mouths.

Such is how the future lives
without influencing the world.
And my mother? She's the girl
hundreds of miles south, blowing
air into a plastic ring skinned

with water and soap. The flimsy
bubbles lift. Whether they are
pushed into a wall, the spikes
of branches, or the sky's blue field,
it is up to the wind.

ACCORDING TO ONE STATISTIC

Fifteen percent of all pregnant women
miscarry, which means the day we slipped

out from our mothers' hips alive
chance was standing in our corner.
Try telling that to my brother when his wife

phoned him at work, punching numbers
with fingers slick and ruby with loss.

Those who were there said a death glow
replaced his fatherly glow, his khakis
and white shirt haloed in black light.

I was there. My eyes fixated
on the cherry bloodstain above his collar

where the razor scraped too close.
Another statistic tells us every minute
there are two hundred fifty births.

By the time my brother arrived home
and called out *Debra, Debra?*

over four thousand babies were born,
four thousand pairs of new lungs
were busy inflating, deflating.

So much screaming added to the world,
so much jubilation now and now and now.

My brother found her buckled.
My brother whisked her to the hospital.
My brother without hope.

And what of the statistics for false alarms?
Here's one. Look how tiny her hands

in the sonogram, how transparent her skin,
her heart a photograph of a stone
skipping across dark water.

He asked to be resurrected as a dolphin
but dolphins were running low on earth
so hours after his final breath shuttled out

from his lungs they wrapped his spirit up
in orange scales instead and transported him
to a pet store aquarium. It's comical

and it's not, considering the lesions
that governed his flesh when he was human,
the static of his wheezing, how his partner

held him long after he turned into a husk.
Then the conversion to goldfish, not the sleek
blue-gray body he always wanted,

one that would allow him to stitch—over
and under and over—the ocean's sequin dress.
Disappointed, but not unlucky

since a loveable boy carried that goldfish
from the store in a clear baggy, knotted
and bulged with water. Carried it home

where the tank waited, an Emperor's pagoda
like a wedding cake rising out of green gravel.
Thirty-six gallons of tranquility.

The dependable snowdrift of food.
And no suffering—the world's shark,
gouging anything that moves beyond the glass.

Three days sick, your eyes wrapped
in red cellophane, the wastebasket

at your bedside clouded with Kleenex.
But somewhere else, hidden inside a crease

in the universe, you're healthy.
Your spleen is back, snug against

your abdomen. Even your mother's alive,
spooning soup into the O of her mouth

while buckets of cancer are lowered
into another's body. The sun is 30 watts

dimmer, the stars staple themselves
backward to the sky. I'm a stranger.

A cameo is all I get. Just seconds down
an elevator with you, your perfume

a scarf I take to the streets, my heart
muttering *what-if, what-if, what-if* . . .

There's always the pit bull
lunging for someone's throat.
There's always the girl sucked
into the shadow of a van
and dumped in a field or the vast
blue of the ocean. And the car
crumpled like foil on the freeway,
the yellow sheet, the vigil
of flares. There's always that.
There's always the plunging bombs,
those wingless birds, silver-beaked,
whistling their death songs.
There's always the bullied kid
with revenge in his backpack.
Always. And there's always
the Christmas tree in flames,
its ornaments softening
like sherbet, in a house with bodies
dreaming under bedcovers.
A cop to chalk circles around
bullet casings. The black widow
and a baby's pudgy arm. The fallen
dominoes of a derailed train.
There's always an epidemic
congealing in the air. There's
always the busy café and someone
in a trench coat with his finger
on the switch. There's always
the man with a 3-inch nail
driven through his skull plate
who says he didn't feel a thing.

TWO

Two men arguing in an alley, their mouths
hole-punched into their moonlit faces.
All this because of that woman leaning
against the wall, skirt like a matador's cape.

Two men yelling, their hard white teeth
biting holes into the air. Leaning
against brick, the woman and her folded
arms, her painted mouth a wedge of apple.

In this alley where men throw punches,
the moon above them is a hole cut
into the night's curtain. The woman lights
a cigarette, her lipstick blemishing the filter.

Tonight, two men are slugging it out
in this potholed alley. Lit by a lamppost
clouded by gnats, the woman's hair
is lava surging over her shoulders.

It ends with one man unscathed, the other
a goatee of blood. Stars pinhole the sky
as the woman holds against her lover's mouth
a handkerchief, blooming into a rose.

The late night revelry carries on and out into the yard.
Black jacket-ed boy kisses black mascara-ed girl.

Down to the basement they go, dark as a raven's wing.
Darker than the spot where two shadows meet.

Some partygoer poured merlot into the deep end.
Ink from a threatened squid bruising the pool.

A lonely figure only presses the piano's obsidian teeth.
Another on the leather couch eating a bag of prunes.

One stoner asks another: *Is it the absence of light or color?*
Back and forth they chew on the adjective like licorice.

Boy leaves with scratches, tires skidmarking the road.
Mascara branching down the weeping girl's cheeks.

Second stoner says: *Dude, I'm telling you it's light.*
Reaches under the skirt of a lampshade to prove his point.

He gave the playground
teeth, a jagged smile
buried under sand.

He gave the playground
grief. At the bottom
of a slide's tilted J

children fell into a mouth
baring teeth, climbed again
the aluminum ladder.

A boy descends, wheat hair
fanning as he falls
palms-first on the sand.

The playground bites,
a scarlet rivulet slides
to his elbow, paint dripping

down a brush handle.
Teeth, the boy shows
the world his teeth,

the bronze of his scream.
Ducks scatter across
the pond, the sand's edge

where the boy's hand
flutters. Red maple leaf
in the teeth of wind.

THE WHIRLING FUNNEL

for Mark

It's me and the man who chased
a man who chased tornadoes.

It's a bar. It's pool balls we knock
around the felt. Says it was

the end of the world, this man
who sat shotgun in a truck

heading toward the whirling funnel.
Says it was colossal. Says it

with eyes lifted and arms spread
like a preacher's. It's physics

how the balls scatter. It's luck when
I make the combo, the bank shot.

Out of the pages of Revelations,
he says. How it ripped the glasses

from a man's face, an infant
from a mother's arms, he says.

It's a black tail whipping houses flat.
It's destiny for those who remain

standing. Rolling where it will
over the green world, it's the eight ball.

Do not be alarmed if you smell smoke.
Which is from the wildfire and not the plane.
From a single match struck by an arsonist
and dropped on the forest floor. Look out
the windows to your right and down below.
That ruin was meant. To dress as many trees
with fire until they have nothing to show
but blackened ribs. When we finally land
and your legs take you outside the airport
the scent of destruction is doubled.
Behind the haze the sun will glow orange
as a jack-o'-lantern in the fog. Click on
the television and this corner of the planet
looks apocalyptic. The tidal wave of flames
and torched houses. A chain-link fence
warped from the heat into a fisherman's net.
All these acres going up brings to mind
the ruin we've made with our own hands.
Ask our exes. Query our skittish children.
If this plane was an air tanker we would skim
the ocean and drape white veils of water
over the flames. As many roundtrips
it takes to douse this inferno. So once again
green could brighten the charcoaled hills.
Until someone else walks into the forest alone.
Whose heart is the red tip of a matchstick
he strikes and strikes in his own darkness.

As a toddler he turned thirty-seven
ants into thirty-seven asterisks
by pinching. During his teens
he pummeled the school mascot
and had the linebackers fleeing
whenever his shadow gouged
the earth. He did other things
to the mascot I won't mention
but will point out the linebackers
flinched at the sound of a sharpener
chewing a pencil into a stake.
On his fortieth birthday he picked
a fight with a mountain and laid
the mountain flat. Don't ask me
how he did this or how he took fists
to the ocean and bruised its waves
or the night he stopped the slow orbit
of the moon with a headlock—
cruelty has nothing to do with logic.
He should've died sooner but
shoved Death so hard to the floor
Death spent an afternoon snapping
his bones back in place. Dying
was to be on his terms and when
he finally perished he pushed
his way into heaven and called God
Sissy and Chump and newer insults
like Helium Head and Asparagus Dick
until He handed over the keys
to the universe. At last on a night
the stars quivered he had the sacred
quill and inkwell to scratch down
the new rules for living on this planet
which to no one's amazement
we are obeying faithfully.

Gone their armor and military uniforms,
their revolvers and engraved swords.
Gone their dignity as one by one
they're shoved on stage: Genghis Khan
in Speedos, his gut bulging above

a tinier bulge. Stalin in a wedding dress
with too much lipstick, too much rouge.
Napoleon's not pushed but rolled
on stage in a baby carriage, diapered
and bonneted. When Hitler arrives

in a frilly pink tutu, you grab the bullhorn
from my hands. *Pirouette!* you shout.
He does. I take the bullhorn back,
press the orange trigger. *Tiptoe to Stalin,*
lift his veil, and plant one. He does.

We take turns with the horn and they
all obey—Genghis Khan changes
Napoleon's diaper, Napoleon rides Stalin
on piggyback, Stalin spanks Hitler,
his tutu quaking like a windblown carnation.

When Mao Tse-tung stumbles out
dressed as Little Bo Peep with a hook
and stuffed sheep under his arm, we wonder
if Nero's next, what sort of getup
Mussolini's in, if Pol Pot's nervous or not.

We wonder who else is milling backstage
when again the heavy red curtain
splits open, a waterfall of blood
spilling over the shoulders of another man
who had the world choking on bones.

You're given a balcony view of the parking lot,
of three boys shackled and chained together.
Boys is accurate. Up here you can make out

their slim build beneath the gray jumpsuits,
acne constellating their foreheads and cheeks.
Fifteen tops, their hair eaten away by clippers.

Of course you speculate. *Which boy thieved?*
Which boy raped? Which boy smothered out
another boy with a gun? The middle kid

looks up and waves hello with a cuffed wrist,
a smirk ruling his face. You keep your hands
pocketed. A man holding keys slides open

the door to a white van, grumbling like thunder.
It's clumsy how they pile in, high-stepping
into the belly of the vehicle, one at a time,

chains rattling. No grace. Just more questions.
Which boy dealt? Which boy mugged?
Which boy was ruined by the boy who waved?

JURY DUTY

Out of the barrel a bullet spirals:
the first fact out of the mouth
of the firearms expert. On the top
page of the notebook I was given
I sketch a bullet, my pencil turning
as I squiggle an arrow corkscrewing
like a spring. Another fact: within
the crisscross of a tire's tread
bullets are lodged the same way
a pebble is found wedged beneath
a boot. Beside his defense lawyer
the boy looked bored, all this talk
about spinning bullets and bullets
spinning around a Goodyear,
a boy the next witness said killed
another boy. Six bullets drilling
into his body, one alone through
the liver and heart. I wrote this down:
1 thru liver/heart. What's the use
of my recording this fact, a doodle
of a bullet whirling? Another
testified and another and the boy
spun side-to-side in his swivel chair,
his face twisting into a yawn.
Only when the verdict was given
days later did he wrench his boredom
from his face like a nylon stocking.
Only then did he shoot every juror
with his eyes, this boy who flew from
the get-go, from point A to point B,
and never stopped spiraling.

BULLET

We see the shadow of a bumblebee.
Fat dot skating the basketball court
where it's skins versus shirts. Benched,

a girl flirts with a boy diamonded
with sweat at the three-point line.
The orange ball's pitched his way,

fingers spread as if pushing a glass door.
Around the girl we see the blue air
blushes when she smiles. Shadow

of the basketball slides to the shadow
of the boy, charcoaling the court.
Curbside, a lustrous car rolls,

a tinted window whines down.
The sky around the girl vibrates red.
The boy shoots and we see the shadow

of the ball on the pavement gliding
toward the circle of the hoop.
We see the revolver but not what zips

out of its barrel, not the broken dash
of its shadow. Another black stitch
pulled from the world's seams.

CHESS MATCH ENDS IN FIGHT

As one opponent calling out checkmate
an hour past midnight could crack a man

already broken and bring allegations
from his tongue, violence to his veins,

bring him to rise and hip-knock the table
so the legs screech, so the pieces quiver

and topple, the bishop a salt shaker
kissed by an elbow, bring him to blows,

to blows, to blows, to grasp the winner
and propel him through plate glass

as if a baptism in geometric water,
so the glass rains and dazzles the floor,

so he emerges from the window stunned,
lacerated, to bring blood and the lilac

breath of night, men with stars pinned
to their chests, handcuffs jingling,

so one's booked, the other's stitched,
the coarse thread lacing up the lesions,

as and so and to bring this to this,
we will be there with our brooms.

THREE

EARLY LESSON

I was evicted from my mother's womb
wearing only a purple scream.
A year later I built my first word
in my throat with a deck of letters

I knocked down with my breath.
Letters I shuffled in kindergarten,
an illustration behind each one.
Apple. Beach ball. Cat. Dalmatian.

Had I looked closer, had I lost my eyes
in the hatch-marks, I would've seen
the apple's core festering with rot.
I would've noticed the beach ball

bleeding air from a pinhole,
a canary feather like a yellow tongue
poking from the cat's mouth,
rabies chewing the spotted dog's brain.

I would've learned how death
hides behind every molecule:
a child dressed for Halloween
wearing a mask of the entire universe.

VONS PARKING LOT, LATE OCTOBER

Piled into a cardboard box
chest-high and this wide,
the pumpkins. What strange

winter squash, orange heads
from a guillotine's afternoon
of severing. This one's

lopsided. That one's
collapsing at the stem
and bearded with black

mold, a housefly
crawling along its equator.
Not a single one

worth lugging home
to cut sockets into its husk,
to knife a crooked smile.

I buy what's penciled
on the list, the front wheel
of my cart squeaking

down the aisles. Back outside
I forget the pumpkins
and watch a man lose his head

inside a trashcan, mining
for aluminum. He comes up
with a face more grime

than skin, his eyes
blue marbles pushed in soil,
and lumbers off

with his plastic bag rattling—
the bones of the dead
bumping each other in the dark.

GHOST BROTHER

There, at the foot of these stairs,
pain dragged its barbed wire

through my mother's stomach
and she buckled, one knee, then

the other, palming her swollen belly.
Brother, I think of you whenever

I hear a gate wheeze open,
whenever I find in a magazine

a black and white illustration
of a pelvis, its wings spread

for flight. I was nine. I didn't
know what miscarriage meant,

a word so heavy my mother
still cannot lift it with her voice.

While she cradled your breath
in her hands, I plucked a butterfly

from her garden before pushing
its spongy abdomen through

the needle of a potted cactus,
pinning it down to this world.

Soon enough, after this slow bend
under the overpass, we will know
the story of this gridlock,
why the red eyes of brake lights
are opening their lids. We ease
around the turn and see the medallion
of the sun, a bonfire in the sky.
Every windshield blinded by gold,
but this is Southern California—
we fish out sunglasses from glove
compartments, purses, shirt pockets.
By the roadside, two cars
shattered by velocity and glare.
Traffic unloosens as the rest of us
accelerate, every car towing
its own rectangular shadow,
the deepest lavender, the hole
of an open grave at dawn—Damn,
it's barely seven a.m. and already
I'm confronted with death.
I dwell on my mortality, theirs,
then mine again. The pros and cons
of coffin and urn. One's too
claustrophobic. The other
you're cooked and cooked
until you're seven pounds of ash.
No wonder some of us believe
in the afterlife, the spirit flitting
in the body, the spirit shuttling off
to heaven after it's unzipped
from the body. Up ahead
our closest star blazes. Bumper
to bumper we make a beeline
toward its light, honeying our skin.
Our sun-warmed and borrowed skin.

Story goes a frozen pond and a stubborn girl
gliding across it, the mirror of her blades
flashing beneath her boots. Story goes

her breath was webbing beyond her mouth.
They warned her not to go there, the story
goes, and now she was, her blades scoring

the oval mirror of the pond. A warning
sign was there, yellow on metal, a black hand
waving under broken ice. Story goes

the pond's moaning was a whale's calling,
was the iron hinge of a wooden door nudged
by wind. *See?* says the girl, her blades etching

zero after zero, the wind tearing the webs
of her breath. *See?* says the pond, cracking
open its crystal mouth, swallowing the girl

whole. Story goes cold, goes into the zero
of ripples, the zero of bubbles, rising up
from a girl who became a story to tell.

Telephone rang and then we knew
of your accident, your death,
your car in a ditch. Stunned

and pushing our bodies forward
into the next day and the next.
Your death, your car in a ditch,

your accident—drifting finally
from our minds at the Cineplex
while the plot spooled out,

while the blue-eyed actor wept
on cue and another argued
with another. Your car in a ditch,

your accident, your death—
forgotten. Until the picture vibrated
and the projector's bulb

sizzled a hole into the filmstrip,
a hole made of light. Not then,
but after. The quiet minutes

of darkness in our plush seats—
then. Your accident, your death,
your car in a ditch coming back

to us the way the movie did,
reeling toward an ending
we never would've guessed.

After the lamb and rice and eggplant
the plates rattled in the sink,
the faucet hissed. Still we had
our wineglasses and buckshots
of laughter. Sleeping on the floor,
the bullmastiff, the largest
of dogs, his coat a dark velvet.
When one of us spoke of her heart's
glitch, how the face of the doctor
bleached with dread, silence tipped
its watering can, pooled.
The table's polished oval held
our reflections. Laughter again
when someone cracked a joke
about the dog's stillness and size:
He looks just like a beanbag.
The host doled out the poker chips,
shuffled and dealt: two down,
one up. So we knew from the start
something about each other.
More wine and more laughter
as the rainbow pillars of our chips
rose and fell. We forgot
about the sleeping dog, how death
turned one of our hearts end-over-
end in his fingers like a poker chip.
Past midnight when we shrugged
into our coats, when something
immense awoke from a long
slumber, brushed past our legs
and out the door, its unclipped nails
clicking against the pavement
like the clock on the wall.

NIGHT

The sun's yolk breaks on the horizon,
the night holding the fork, the night
with its assembly of stars. Now,
when the bedroom's upholstered
with shadows, is when I think of the dead.
Now, as the moon hangs full, as a moth
knocks its wings against a porch bulb.

A quarter past ten, the world outside
like underexposed film, and my wife
is on the freeway. Headlights swivel,
side-door crunch, car horn stuck
blaring its single brassy note—
forgive me for imagining the worst.
It's this darkness. Birds mute in the trees.

Night, you hangman's hood, scuffed
leather boot, hand-me-down dress.
You tar pit, vulture wing, stain—
bring my wife safely home and I promise
to love you again. Every shade of black,
every star turning slowly over my head,
riding the Ferris wheel of the heavens.

Another sunset and enamored couple
to row down these canals, sky blushing

and the water teal, the twin pistons
of my arms pushing us under another bridge,

another kiss. Three months on the job
and this close to hanging up my oars,

torching my beret and jailer-striped shirt,
what with all the smooching and romance,

my own love life nothing but tossed seeds
down a shower drain, a porn actress

thrashing behind closed eyelids.
My favorite part of the ride is this:

when I motion to the house on our right,
the outdoor spiral staircase that coils

from bedroom to grass, when I tell them
the man who built this for his wife

lost his wife. They always sigh, like this
loving pair, pulling their bodies closer

as we slowly glide forward, the sun
gone now, the sky dusted with stars.

See how quiet they get, how death shoves
a gag inside their mouths? You can tell

they're wondering whose heart will stop
drumming first, which body will climb

down the staircase from bedroom to grass
to underground, the earth filling in the space

that body had been. I paddle our way
back to the dock, tie off the gondola and help

the woman out first, then her husband,
my lantern yellowing their faces. I pocket

his folded bill as they stroll down the pier,
the evening cold enough to witness

their breathing like clouds of chalk
when two erasers are clapped together.

Exhume your heart. Put the bleeding thing
inside a Ziploc, inside the freezer.
Pocket your wedding band and drive

to the nearest bar. Have a drink.
Have another. Make conversation
with the woman with fishnet stockings

mapping the topography of her legs.
Be charming. Say *A blind man*
could fall in love with your eyes.

Say *I want to memorize the alphabet*
of your body. Have one more drink
at her apartment. Compliment her

on the décor, the zebra-striped couch,
the lava lamp in the corner of her bedroom
juggling its organs in slow-motion.

Kiss. Unclasp her bra, unloosen your belt,
varnish her skin with your tongue.
Do what you came there to do.

Get dressed, go home, pretend nothing
happened. When your wife finds it
in the freezer the morning after,

when she asks *What is this?* say *Dinner.*
Let it thaw all day on the kitchen counter.
Listen to it shushing on the grill.

Of unruly patients she spoke, tossed bedpans
and teeth-marked wrists. Of the quiet man

who shredded his nose with only his fingers,
of the hospital bed where his wife swabbed

around the triangular hole above his mouth.
That's love, I told the nurse at her apartment.

It's something, she replied. Once more
I tipped the bottle and filled her wineglass,

filled my own, our heads rising and dipping
like buoys. And our bodies too as we weaved

into her bedroom wallpapered in darkness.
Afterwards, while her breathing scratched

the quiet, I imagined bits of cartilage
under the man's fingernails, and the woman

who stood by her husband while his face
slowly turned into a Greek statue's—

Dionysus in marble, his nose lopped off
by the mallet of time. Bedsprings whined

in the morning when I rose, harsh light
in the bathroom. Above the giant eye socket

of the sink, my face was pale as Styrofoam.
Leaving the nurse was an exercise in stealth.

I had to make my head vanish, my torso
and limbs. *There*, I said with my ghost

tongue, my ghost throat and vocal chords,
and walked out with legs made of air.

FOUR

PORTRAIT OF MY FATHER SLAPPING HIS EAR

The lucid minutes after he lost his job
my father leans in the back yard

on one blue-jeaned leg, his sunlit face
a Cézanne peach

tilted on his shoulders. On the phone
they told him. Now this leaning

with back arched, with a hand
lifted to his crimson ear—

No, he's not listening
to the wind's sermon on loss

or eavesdropping on the clouds.
What we have here is a honeybee

mistaking the spiral and fold
of a man's ear

for a rose, how that simple accident
makes my father corkscrew

like this, bend one leg,
his shadow question-marking the grass.

Makes his hand
slap the noise drilling into his skull,

his hand blurred, the noise
gold. They told him on the phone,

then the dial tone's droning.
Afterwards, the back yard,

the leaning, the confusion
of a bee looking for nectar.

Torn cardboard and a black Sharpie
were all he needed to proclaim a jungle

swallowed him three decades ago
and spit him out with the memory

of bullets perforating leaves and flesh.
However this didn't coax enough hands

to wave bills outside their car windows
so the next day he fashioned a new sign:

Visions of a hamburger. Some had
translated this as *Visions of a hangover*

without entertaining the thought
of a Big Mac suspended and glowing

halolike above his head. More people
accelerated than he would've liked

so he came up with: *Lost my job,
my home, my snugglebug.* That failed

as well, as did: *Honk if you're housing
cobwebs inside your purse/wallet.*

Call it luck, the final words he shuffled
together that cracked opened the husks

of their hearts: *HEY YOU silhouetted
behind windows dark as film negative*

with the sun dazzling off alloy rims—
Camus once said, "Charm is a way

of getting the answer yes without
asking a clear question," which is true

in most social situations, but here
on this corner, sporting this jacket

exhumed from a trash bin, these shoes
held together by the mercy of duct tape‽

And you over there behind the wheel,
sealed-in and cooled by the icy breath

of your AC as you wait for the ~~yellow~~
red eye of the traffic light to downturn

to emerald, you who wish to be
remembered as a good, honest person

(which you are!) when your body
belly-ups and this beautiful world

covers you with forty blankets of soil‽
My charisma can only do so much.

By *island* I mean this narrow stretch of lawn
dividing the road, a boulder here and here,
little trees with trunks thick as broom handles.

By *man* I mean the one pushing the mower
with a red bandana wound around his head,
his face enameled in sweat. A wind-up toy,

he goes forward and back, the mower growling
before him, chewing the grass. The sun
won't quit. It slams its heat against the world.

It makes chrome dazzle, the unshaded squint,
and broils this man on an island surrounded
not by water but tar, by cars gliding north-

and southbound, quick as sharks. Who knows
what his message in a bottle would be, what plea
on a scrolled wrapper in an empty Corona

lying in the gutter. Something about his rent,
his roof. Something about minimum wage.
A crude map of the city, an X where he works:

this island we drive by and drive by and drive by.

On her lawn the juniper evolved and shears
was all she needed. Shears and the eye to see
a grizzly inside the hedges, a kangaroo inside
the grizzly, a squirrel inside the kangaroo.
While she pruned and clipped, the blonde vines
of her son's hair lengthened to his shoulders.
Heavy metal thundered out from his window
and into the neighborhood. Guitars yelped
in the trees. A drum solo clamored
inside the Jones's tin and red-flagged mailbox.
Then the rattletraps that idled before her house,
the folded bills swapped for a plastic baggie
slipped through a hole in the wooden fence
where a knot once spiraled. While she trimmed
and snipped. While the shears *tsk-tsked*
down the leafy limbs, around the green snout—
another sculpted animal we could recognize.

The firecracker of my father's
knuckles on my door and out
the window I go, with cowlicks
and cigarettes and a can
of spray paint. I'm on my bike,
I'm two wheels and a blue frame,
I'm tunneling through wind
until I'm here, the graveyard
of impounded cars, doors dented
and doors scabbed with rust.
A rock's all I need to crochet
with cracks a doily on a windshield.
Then the rattle of the can,
the long hiss as I deface a Pontiac
with the vines of my angst.
Once this was all a revelation.
Once vandalism was a spoonful
of adrenaline dumped into my blood.
Now my heart ticks away,
unmoved. Inside a junked car
I light up, press the glowing ash
into the butterscotch leather.
The charred holes in the upholstery
remind me of Zoe's moles.
Gone, six Midwest states away,
but not before she pushed a needle
into a Bic, pushed her initials
into my arm. Gone the scent
of her, the marijuana and vanilla
of her. Gone her pierced
bottom lip and aquamarine hair,
the way it whipped around
inside her convertible, wave
after wave crashing on her forehead—

those seatbeltless days we flew
into a world that kicked
our hearts so hard with its beauty
it always left a bruise.

BALCONY TALK WITH CIGARS

for Ernie

Smoke blurs our faces as we go back and forth:
what we fired as boys, what we used to fire it.

Here he is with a marble and a slingshot.
Here I am with my aluminum bat, a jar

of nuts and bolts, the chime of metal on metal.
Now him, swinging crab apples off the end

of a sharpened stick, their trajectories
souring the air. Now me, feeding the sky

unripe lemons with a tennis racket, the dull thud
of each whack, one hard fruit after another

shrinking to green periods. We go back
and forth like this. What we fired.

What we used to fire it. Catapulted pine cones,
pennies flicked out a car window, pitching

rocks into a wheat field with a 9-iron.
Above us, stars push thumbtacks into the night.

Three floors below on the curb, an empty
metal trashcan. And this is how we toast

the Saint of Boyish Behavior once more:
I lean over the railing, fling my cigar—

comet dust sizzling out on the road.
Now him. The careful aim, the perfect lob—

burst of orange sparks in the trashcan
ringing like a church bell muffled by distance.

This is the garage, the place he squandered
seasons pitching darts behind a chalked

line, eying the bull's-eye. Days of flinging
and retrieving, four steps forward, four back,

because he didn't know what else to do,
misguided as he was, snagged as he was.

Time didn't budge, the circular board
a clock where he nailed the minute hand

like a pinned insect. Read the wall's Braille,
pinholes meant for double twenty or sixteen,

and you will know the story of his failures.
One hole's for the job he couldn't hold,

one for the footprints of his wife's departure.
This one's for the fistfight that turned

his face into a raccoon's. And this one here
which barely missed the dartboard

is the hole that keeps opening under his feet.
Now he always hits what he aims for,

sure thing again and again, pin the tail
on the donkey minus the blindfold.

So early he awoke in the morning for this,
so late he stayed up working the oiled hinge

of his elbow until summer hoarded its heat
and dragged it elsewhere, until his aim

was a thing to marvel: dead-on, flawless,
nothing he could repeat in his life.

DUMBEST

Drilling through my finger's not the dumbest thing I've done.
BOB HICOK

Have I ever told you about the hickey
I self-inflicted on my forehead? Fifteen

and bored, greenbottle flies tapping between
the window and screen, and I found

a suction cup to play with. Nothing
like the anguish of a drill bit burrowing

through flesh, but a bandaged finger
looks cooler than a scarlet sun setting

on a brow ridge. For two days I wore
the mark of stupidity, two days and nights

I wore bangs. There are degrees of dumb,
and I say a holey finger's smarter

than a circle of burst capillaries
on the forehead, yet both are genius

compared to the farmer and his friends
I read about. They drank and drank,

which led to shucking off their clothes
and slamming frozen turnips against

their heads, which led to someone
chainsawing the end of his foot to prove

he was most macho. I imagine no one
knew how to shut the faucet of blood,

laughter gushing from their throats,
that someone pointed at the piggies

lying in the snow. Wait, it gets dumber,
and by dumber I mean the farmer held

the buzzing saw to his jugular and said,
Watch this. No one chuckled after that.

Not one dumbfounded drunk, not the one
who unhinged his head from his neck.

Bob, promise you won't approach
a frozen gas-cap with a lighter again

and I promise I won't approach
a bullet with a ball-peen hammer again.

If a dangerous idea presses the buzzer,
let's ask Reason to answer the door.

Here's the alternative: your beloved
crumpled on the carpet, my darling

wiping her swollen eyes, both muttering
under their own breaths, *Stupid, stupid.*

The oversized pink donut fashioned on the roof
reminds me of the hole in the ozone dilating

above Antarctica, above the clueless penguins
wobbling over blue ice. Gets me thinking about

rings and holes in general, a life preserver tossed
from a yacht into the frothing waters where

someone's head once bobbed. About inner tubes
and nooses. About halos, glowing like white neon

over the heads of angels swarming around
a benevolent being. Benevolent and powerless

or else another day for the man consumed by waves
to sip a martini on deck. Or else merciful hands

to stitch closed the ozone's wound. Ergo,
God's a hole in the sky, big as the O in Oblivion.

To get from *I don't believe* to *I believe* one must
jump through many hoops garlanded with flames.

Or one hoop, unlit and inches off the ground.
I don't know. My reasoning has more holes

than a colander as I wobble across the iceberg
of life's meaning, clueless as the next guy

who happens to be stepping out of the donut shop
carrying a dozen. Wish I had one. Glazed

or chocolate. One that dusts my lips and powders
the floor like snow shaken off a crow's wings.

THE EYES

Forever our eyes are grabbing.
Be it what a windshield brackets,

be it the television's onslaught:
collie in mid-air snapping hold

onto a Frisbee, a magnified
razor shearing off a black forest

of stubbles, and so on. Then
a wildfire's eating the hills,

a weatherman points to a storm
pinwheeling around an eye

that never blinks. A book,
the eyes love a book, following

every word's inked footprint
from margin to margin.

Museums too, how the eyes
sponge over a Miró or Klee,

the ice cream and bubblegum
hues of a de Kooning. Let's not

forget the movies, a hotspot
for the eyes, so many lifted

from darkness to a screen
illuminated by the car chase,

a bedsheet's heave and fall,
the orange rose of an explosion.

Sometimes the eyes are fooled,
trompe l'oeil they call it,

a brick wall that's really a wall
with painted on bricks.

Or the eyes just quit, a shadow
swallows them like a pair of dice

in a velvet bag. Tell me how
she does it, this woman skimming

the sidewalk with a white cane,
eyes sunk behind shades?

In the directory she's mapped
in her mind, it says *You Are Here*

wherever she stands. But where
are we when a benevolent hand

brushes our eyelids closed
for good? Let me start this over:

For now our eyes are grabbing . . .

FIVE

FONTANELLE

In the womb our skull's not one bone
but pieces of bone. It's plate tectonics
how they come together. It's jigsaw.
Except here, the gap where four
rounded corners don't quite meet.

Soft spot, it bulges when the baby
weeps, sinks when he's dehydrated.
Mostly it pulsates, as if beneath
those silky filaments of first hair
the cranium protects a heart instead.

Who hasn't once imagined pushing
their finger through the dome,
poking the gray matter? Dark thought,
plum on my thumb, my own scalp
shivers just thinking about it.

One to two years, the skull's trapdoor
closes. Finally the brain's protected.
Except here, this entrance to the theater
of the mind. Doorway for any
bad idea or influence to walk through

and take the plush seat beside us.
How thrilling infidelity becomes then.
How sensible it sounds to leap
from a bridge into oblivion. Here:
this opening I cannot put my finger on.

EPISODE

His head *jackknifed* is the best way to put it.
She sliced the teakettle's throat when it screeched
on the burner. After the water was poured, the air
above the teacup filled with ghost shavings.

His head swayed on the ceiling like a birthday balloon.
Outside, a windblown potted plant sliced
the air with long green knives. You could see
the moon was quickly becoming a ghost.

The moon with its head inside the night's guillotine.
A lemon slice to squeeze into the tea. He blew
steam into the air before taking a sip.
A ghost-cloud pressed its face against the window

as his head slowly descended back into his collar.
With the bedroom light sliced off, the dark arrived—
a black crayon scribbling over air. His face
was ghostlike. There, where the crayon stopped filling.

A man collapses in the snow.
Hours later he awakens, bewildered,
the corners of his face—nosetip,

cheekbones—blackened by frostbite.
Hypothermia bends the compass needle
in his brain as a rescue team emerges

from the white haze. No,
five trees with their backs turned
against the blizzard. Before death

swallows his heart like a cherry,
a chopper arrives. After the airlift,
the scrolling credits, I turn off the TV

and take a Paxil with a cup of water.
Somewhere inside my body
the first snowflake catches

on the eyelash of depression.
In fifteen minutes the snow flurry
of calm will bury him completely.

It is this moment I enjoy the most.
When his heartbeat almost stops.
Before he survives.

THE CIRCUS OCTOPUS

> When the circus was disbanded, the octopus was kept in a tank and no
> one paid any attention to his tricks. He gradually lost color (octopuses'
> states of mind are expressed in their shifting hues) . . . and used his beak
> to stab himself so badly that he died.
>
> > ANDREW SOLOMON,
> > from *The Noonday Demon*

After the clowns erased their faces
with a box of Kleenex.
Wiped their painted brows

and mouths, little Kandinskys
on squares of tissue.
After the clowns went home

and the stakes were wrenched
from the earth. Yanked so the tent
could deflate, could become

a jellyfish collapsed on the shore.
After the clowns, the deflated tent,
there was the tank to consider,

the strange creature inside
changing hues. To consider
the glass coffin of the tank,

what to do with a creature
with eight arms, three hearts,
color draining from the alien head.

What eerie thought budding there
behind the unblinking eye.
What colorless dread.

A short fellow, a matted-beard man,
hair wild and eyes wilder, lapis blue
and darting here there, here there.
Lugging a guitar case or a bag
of aluminum, the black scissors
of his shadow clipping at his heels,
dirty socks or sockless, raincoat
or moth-eaten sweater, sleeves full
of mouths. Sometimes the violent
thrust of arms, hands slapping
wind, the invisible butterflies,
sometimes a head-jerk, a twitch
scurrying across his face like a roach
beneath the sheets. I've seen him
on the highway, on the off-ramp,
flinching on 2nd, lamenting on 4th,
the liquor store across from where
I live, talking back to the buzzing
Coke machine, one voice or more
riding the carousel of his brain.
Meds might help, a coin might
flip, beard clipped short and hair
disciplined by a comb, mind clear
as the heavens stretched from Kansas
to Montana. Instead he gets a head
he shakes like a snow globe,
blizzard after blizzard, salvation
of a miniature cabin in the glass
dome, two windows painted yellow,
the front door missing a knob.

APPOINTMENT

The leather couch like a beached whale.
On the wall a clock grinds its teeth.

A headache tightens its clamp
on my psychiatrist's temples and he says

If you don't mind, I'd like to cut
this session short. In five minutes

I paraphrase my troubles, how calm
I feel until I wake up in the morning

wearing anxiety's wool T-shirt.
Try taking the pills at night, he says.

At home I straighten books on a shelf.
I flip through a magazine and stop

at a photograph of a man removing
his prosthetic nose. Outside, the sun drags

its feet, weary of another engagement
with the dark side of the world.

SELF-PORTRAIT WITH BACK TURNED

At this angle, you don't know if I'm making
a face or not. Have a nosebleed or don't.

If I'm holding a robin's egg inside my mouth
or my mouth is empty. Forgive me for closing

myself to you with the coffee-brown curtain
of my hair. I've done this before with a door.

I've done it with silence, swinging it like a door
in the face of the baffled. I'm winking one eye

or not. Shaved my beard or didn't. I'm chewing
on a toothpick or my teeth are unoccupied.

Pardon me for holding my tongue, for not
revealing this dark thing perched in my head

with clipped wings, its black feathers
side by side on the floor like an open quote.

A BRIEF HISTORY OF ANTIDEPRESSANTS

My life a bombed site turning green again.
FRANZ WRIGHT

Let's begin with the black
wind coiling inside Mother's

skull, the iron gate banging
through her nights. That

and the days she hovered
above her body, a kite

lifted airborne by a gust
the color of shadow—

darker, even.
The doctor spooled

her down, swiftly
signed the prescription

for Elavil. Lovely word,
Elavil—how the tongue

touches the mouth's roof,
lets go, touches again.

Two weeks medicated
before the hallucinations:

here's a spider
the size of a human head

inching up the wall.
Here's an empty

rocking chair, leaning
forward and back,

forward, back. Enough
for her to flush the pills,

to invite back into her head
the wind's dark churning.

✦

I was born with a rabid dog
chewing on my bones,

with a heart swinging
on a meat hook.

I was born with a bad idea
knocking on my brain:

See that ledge? See
the X-acto blade's fang

salivating over your wrist?
I was born with noise.

✦

Gwendolyn knows
them all—Wellbutrin

and Effexor, Lithium
and Celexa. Knows

the song each one
serenades to her blood.

And this is how
she scales her moods:

one to ten. One's
a head full of nightmare,

a gang of vultures
dismantling her thoughts.

Ten means she's been
kissed by rapture, means

sunlight in her veins,
a radiant heart.

Tonight, Gwendolyn
says, *I'm only a seven,*

her voice deflating
in her throat. Nowhere

near those dreadful birds
picking apart her mind.

Just three states away
from bliss, but no bus ticket

to take her there,
no truck driver to answer

her thumb's plea for a lift,
aimed toward heaven.

✦

Describe the sensation.
My head was a helium balloon.

What was that screeching?
The kettle on the burner.

Talk about the steam.
It spiraled like ghost shavings.

Who poured the tea?
Girlfriend then, wife now.

What happened next?
The balcony whispered my name.

Go back to the balloon.
Someone snipped the thread.

How long were you detached?
Until the hour hand fingered 10.

What did your head do?
Drift back into my collar.

And the bedroom where you slept?
Dyed with evening.

You mentioned your wife's voice.
A sewing needle, mending, mending.

◆

I know an anguished girl
thin as a broom handle,

bale of dark hair, two drops
of Pacific for eyes.

Was anguished, I mean.
Was an orange-tailed fox gnawing

on her hind leg. It took a week
of the morning ritual,

of capsule, water glass,
and blue swallowing.

Now the steel trap's empty,
the snow's dimpled by

paw prints, every fourth
depression glowing red.

✦

Praise my beloved
for driving me to Branko's,

the shortcut she knows
so well. Praise his couch,

his first question—
What's troubling you,

young man? Praise the jeweled
necklace of speech, the way

my tongue rolled over each
beaded word: *I* and *don't*

and *know,* then *where* and *to*
and *start.* Praise the pills

the color of flamingoes.
Praise their flight to my mouth.

✦

So amazed I was
at the aquarium—

in that darkened room
I entered like a cave,

behind walls of glass,
the ballet of jellyfish—

I forgot that evening
the chalky pink tablet.

From tank to tank
I glided, gazed in awe

each species, the ones
that opened and closed

their crystal umbrellas,
ones that mushroomed

like fallen bombs
before imploding back

into their ghostly bodies.
Yes, so dazzled I was

when I slipped my body
under the covers, I forgot

my pill, unswallowed
on the nightstand

as evening pooled
and flooded the bedroom,

as my mind drifted
back to the aquarium—

all those luminous hearts
pulsing in black water.